NEW
BABY

SURVIVAL
GUIDE

TRANSLATION GUIDE

We are two British mums/moms with three boys each, so we have lots of experience of changing nappies/diapers before putting baby into a babygrow/romper/sleepsuit, settling them with a dummy/pacifier and taking them for a walk in their pram/pushchair/buggy.

Our words and spellings may differ from yours, but we believe many aspects of motherhood are the same— and especially our need to spend time with the Lord and to trust our newborn baby into his care.

New Baby Survival Guide
© Cassie Martin and Sarah Smart/The Good Book Company, 2013

Published by The Good Book Company
Tel (UK): 0333 123 0880
International: +44 (0) 208 942 0880
email: info@thegoodbook.co.uk

UK: www.thegoodbook.co.uk
North America: www.thegoodbook.com
Australia: www.thegoodbook.com.au
New Zealand: www.thegoodbook.co.nz

ISBN (Blue): 9781909559813 ISBN (Pink): 9781909559110

Design by André Parker

Printed in China

CONTENTS

Welcome to the wonderful world of parenting! With three boys each, we understand the wave of "Aaaaaaaaaagh!!!" that threatens to drown new mums. As Christians, the dreaded "Quiet Time" with your Bible also looms in the background—inducing those pesky twins born to all mothers: guilt and inadequacy.

Church becomes a struggle. If we made it, we were usually elsewhere during the sermon (in mind and/or body). Nappy changing, crying (baby and/or you), and dreading whipping your breasts out publicly can leave you alone in some dingy backroom, covered in various bodily excrements and running mascara, needing to GO HOME. Hormonal minds and practical chaos conspire. When people encourage us with "You're Supermum", we check our knickers aren't on over our trousers.

We ask friends: "Pray for our Quiet Times". Sympathy abounds but, from kind motives, not much gentle challenging to re-establish good habits. Of course, we will all have days when we miss time in God's word or fall asleep mid-prayer, but when days turn into months, it becomes unhelpful and ultimately sinful.

2 Timothy 3 v 16-17 is brilliant:

> *"All Scripture is God-breathed and is useful for teaching, rebuking, correcting and training in righteousness, so that the servant of God may be thoroughly equipped for every good work."*

We need thorough equipping in the good work of motherhood. Being equipped doesn't mean owning a gold-plated buggy or knowing what time the latest guru advises I cut my toenails. Equipping means reading the Bible.

So, here's a survival guide, which is do-able and God-centred. There's probably no time, brainpower or energy for your usual "solids" but: "Like newborn babies, crave pure spiritual milk, so that by it you may grow up in your salvation" (1 Peter 2 v 2).

These studies are aimed for those moments when you can quickly Bible-dip. God longs to speak to you. When those five minutes come, pray for the spiritual discipline to take them. Don't feel guilty. Some days it just won't happen. That's OK. God loves us because of Jesus' death, not because of our "Quiet Time Quota". As his beloved children, he loves us even more than you love your precious newborn.

CASSIE AND SARAH

P.S. These studies are best consumed with chocolate...

01.
REST FOR
YOUR SOUL

PSALM 116 v 1-9

[1] I love the LORD, for he heard my voice;
    he heard my cry for mercy.

[2] Because he turned his ear to me,
    I will call on him as long as I live.

[3] The cords of death entangled me,
    the anguish of the grave came over me;
    I was overcome by distress and sorrow.

[4] Then I called on the name of the LORD:
    "LORD, save me!"

[5] The LORD is gracious and righteous;
    our God is full of compassion.

[6] The LORD protects the unwary;
    when I was brought low, he saved me.

[7] Return to your rest, my soul,
    for the LORD has been good to you.

[8] For you, LORD, have delivered me from death,
    my eyes from tears,
    my feet from stumbling,

[9] that I may walk before the LORD
    in the land of the living.

The Anglican Prayer Book uses this psalm in its prayer of thanksgiving after childbirth—and you can see why! However long or traumatic your experience of giving birth, the Lord was with you in it.

- How bad were things for the writer of this psalm (v 3)?
- Who did he turn to (v 4)?
- Why (v 1-2 and 5-6)?

In the Lord, we find rest for our souls (v 7), even if we feel far from rested physically! He has been good to us, both in our recent experience of childbirth and above all in bringing us to new spiritual birth; truly delivering us from death (v 8).

••

Thank you, Lord, for a safe delivery and for being with me through the birth of my child(ren). Help me to find rest in you, the One who delivers me from death. Amen

02.
A THANK-OFFERING

PSALM 116 v 10-19

[10] I trusted in the LORD when I said,
"I am greatly afflicted";
[11] in my alarm I said, "Everyone is a liar."
[12] What shall I return to the LORD
for all his goodness to me?
[13] I will lift up the cup of salvation
and call on the name of the Lord.
[14] I will fulfil my vows to the LORD
in the presence of all his people.
[15] Precious in the sight of the LORD
is the death of his faithful servants.
[16] Truly I am your servant, LORD;
I serve you just as my mother did;
you have freed me from my chains.
[17] I will sacrifice a thank-offering to you
and call on the name of the LORD.
[18] I will fulfil my vows to the LORD
in the presence of all his people,
[19] in the courts of the house of the LORD—
in your midst, Jerusalem.
Praise the LORD.

The first half of Psalm 16 focuses on what the Lord has done for the psalm writer. In this half, we see the writer's response.

- **o** What question does he ask himself (v 12)?
- **o** Can we ever do that?
- **o** How *can* we respond (v 16-17)?

Although people can let you down (v 11), the Lord never will. He is unfailingly good (v 12), graciously gives us salvation (v 13), and keeps us even through death (v 15).

So even if a health professional lets you down, your husband snores through the 3am feed and your own reserves of patience run out, the Lord is enough. Praise the Lord.

....

Heavenly Father, thank you that this psalm writer vows to serve you as his mother did. I pray that my child will learn from me how wonderful and good you are, and that they in turn will long to serve you in gratitude. Amen

03.
SERVING IN
THE SMALL HOURS

PSALM 134
A SONG OF ASCENTS

¹ Praise the LORD, all you servants
    of the LORD
    who minister by night in the house
    of the LORD.
² Lift up your hands in the sanctuary
    and praise the LORD.
³ May the LORD bless you from Zion,
    he who is the Maker of heaven
    and earth.

Woo hoo! You've done it: you've read a *whole* psalm! This psalm is about God's ministers leading their people by example in worshipping him. You are a God-appointed minister to your child.

Ministering simply means to meet someone's needs—spiritual, physical, practical and emotional. You'll be doing a lot of ministering by night! Be encouraged; it's all service to, and seen by, God.

- o As the Lord's servant, what are you called to do (v 1)?
- o "Lift up your hands" (v 2) is an Old Testament phrase for praying.
  What should our prayers include?

Verse 3 reassures us that God is the almighty Maker of heaven and earth… and of your baby. God longs to bless those who praise him.

....

Praise you, Lord, that you are the Maker of everything. Thank you for appointing me to minister to my child. Give me patience and joy, particularly at night. Help me to lead my child in a praise and prayer-filled life. Amen

04.
LIFT UP THOSE BLEARY EYES!

PSALM 121 v 1-4
A SONG OF ASCENTS

¹ I lift up my eyes to the mountains—
  where does my help come from?
² My help comes from the LORD,
  the Maker of heaven and earth.
³ He will not let your foot slip—
    he who watches over you will not
      slumber;
⁴ indeed, he who watches over Israel
    will neither slumber nor sleep.

⁵ The LORD watches over you—
    the LORD is your shade at your right
      hand;
⁶ the sun will not harm you by day,
    nor the moon by night.
⁷ The LORD will keep you from all harm—
    he will watch over your life;
⁸ the LORD will watch over your coming
      and going
    both now and for evermore.

Picture the Jews making their way to Jerusalem for a feast. The journey would have been mountainous, hard and dangerous. They're singing this psalm after a long journey; exhausted, muscles aching, thankful for God's help through trouble. Sound familiar?

- Verse 1 acknowledges that we need help (when we lift our eyes up to the mountains... of washing). Where does that help come from (v 2)?
- Why is he able to help us?
- How are these verses reassuring to you as a new mother (v 3-4)?

Often, as mothers, we can be over-anxious about our babies, particularly when they're sleeping. Rest assured: God looks after us and watches our babies constantly. His people are safe in his care. Nothing happens that is outside his loving purposes.

....

Lord, thank you that even though you are the Maker of heaven and earth, you are my help, always watching over my children. Amen

05.
DESIGNER
SHADES

PSALM 121 v 5-8
A SONG OF ASCENTS

1 I lift up my eyes to the mountains—
    where does my help come from?
2 My help comes from the Lord,
    the Maker of heaven and earth.
3 He will not let your foot slip—
    he who watches over you will not
        slumber;
4 indeed, he who watches over Israel
    will neither slumber nor sleep.

5 The Lord watches over you—
    the Lord is your shade at your right
        hand;
6 the sun will not harm you by day,
    nor the moon by night.
7 The Lord will keep you from all harm—
    he will watch over your life;
8 the Lord will watch over your coming
        and going
    both now and for evermore.

o What does God do? When is he watching over us (v 5-6)?

o Does verse 7 mean we will never experience problems?

o What is it teaching us?

o How does verse 8 reassure us about our children's future?

These verses do not say that we or our children will not experience troubles, but that we are at all times accompanied, ruled and protected by God and preserved from evil.

Our definition of "harm" may be different from God's. Are you as concerned about your child experiencing spiritual harm as physical harm?

• •

Father, thank you for being constantly beside me. I praise you for your continual protection and watchfulness. Please keep me and my children safe in your love and following you always.

I pray for _____ experiencing difficulties. May they know you watch over them and are their loving Protector. Amen

06.
FIRM
FOUNDATIONS

PSALM 127
A SONG OF ASCENTS.
OF SOLOMON.

¹ Unless the LORD builds the house,
  the builders labour in vain.
  Unless the LORD watches over the city,
  the guards stand watch in vain.
² In vain you rise early
  and stay up late,
  toiling for food to eat—
  for he grants sleep to those he loves.
³ Children are a heritage from the LORD,
  offspring a reward from him.
⁴ Like arrows in the hands of a warrior
  are children born in one's youth.
⁵ Blessed is the man
  whose quiver is full of them.
  They will not be put to shame
  when they contend with their
  opponents in court.

As a new mum, you have years of building blocks and *Lego* in front of you! Without firm foundations (built by somebody who knows what they are doing!) collapse is inevitable.

o What things can we do "in vain" (v 1-2)?
o What does the Lord do (v 1-3)?

Notice how Solomon, the writer of this psalm, describes children: a heritage from the Lord, a reward, a blessing. Not a right or a burden!

•••

Please help me always to see my child(ren) as a gift and blessing from you, Lord. Please may my son/daughter grow up to be someone who lives with you as the foundation of his/her life. Amen

Pray for people you know who are labouring and toiling their way through life without the Lord. Pray for them to recognise the folly and frustration of living without God. Ask God for opportunities to speak about the blessing of living in relationship with him.

07.
HUMBLE
PIE

PSALM 131 v 1
A SONG OF ASCENTS. OF DAVID.

¹ My heart is not proud, LORD,
   my eyes are not haughty;
   I do not concern myself with great
      matters
   or things too wonderful for me.

² But I have calmed and quietened myself,
   I am like a weaned child with its mother;
   like a weaned child I am content.
³ Israel, put your hope in the LORD
   both now and for evermore.

As I opened this psalm, my dribbling cat promptly sat on my Bible and my six-year-old was regaling me with shark jokes; a fitting setting in which to (try to) read verse 1. In your glamorous world of poo, vomit, haemorrhoids (if you're really lucky), and disposable knickers, you can probably relate to this verse too. But what does David actually mean by great and wonderful matters?

○ What does David say about himself (v 1a)?
○ Why is it crucial to let God master our pride?

Pride affects everything adversely. This psalm is one of the easiest to read, but its lesson of total humility before God is one of the hardest to learn.

○ Deuteronomy 29 v 29 says: "The secret things belong to the Lord … but the things revealed belong to us and to our children." How does this help us understand verse 1b?
○ Are you content to trust God, even when you don't understand his purposes?

••

Father, may I not concern myself with your hidden purposes, but trust in your loving will and what I know from the Bible. Please use motherhood to deepen my humility. Amen

08.
WEANING
TECHNIQUES

PSALM 131 V 2-3
A SONG OF ASCENTS. OF DAVID.

¹ My heart is not proud, LORD,
　　my eyes are not haughty;
　I do not concern myself with great
　　　matters
　　or things too wonderful for me.

² But I have calmed and quietened myself,
　　I am like a weaned child with its mother;
　　like a weaned child I am content.
³ Israel, put your hope in the LORD
　　both now and for evermore.

Weaning may seem a long way off, but perhaps you're already looking forward to dropping some of the milk feeds and teaching your little one independent eating/face smearing!

○ How does David describe himself (v 2)?
○ Why do you think he uses (and repeats) the word "weaned"?

Weaning can be a difficult process for a baby, as they move from the milk they have always known to new tastes, textures and techniques, but it is crucial for child development. David has been weaned off his pride—he has literally calmed and quietened himself. A hard process, but essential to spiritual growth.

○ What is the solid food he now finds contentment in (v 3)?

....

Lord, thank you that only you give true contentment and eternal hope. I pray for _____ , who does not know the joy and peace of being your contented child. May they put their hope in you. Amen

09.
OUR ALL-
KNOWING GOD

PSALM 139 v 1-6
FOR THE DIRECTOR OF MUSIC.
OF DAVID. A PSALM.

¹ You have searched me, LORD,
    and you know me.
² You know when I sit and when I rise;
    you perceive my thoughts from afar.
³ You discern my going out and my lying
      down;
    you are familiar with all my ways.
⁴ Before a word is on my tongue
    you, LORD, know it completely.
⁵ You hem me in behind and before,
    and you lay your hand upon me.
⁶ Such knowledge is too wonderful for me,
    too lofty for me to attain.

⁷ Where can I go from your Spirit?
    Where can I flee from your presence?
⁸ If I go up to the heavens, you are there;
    if I make my bed in the depths, you
      are there.
⁹ If I rise on the wings of the dawn,

if I settle on the far side of the sea,
^{10} even there your hand will guide me,
your right hand will hold me fast.

- **o** How is God's perfect knowledge relevant to us, personally (v 1-4)?
- **o** God's intimate knowledge of us and our lives could seem intrusive and scary, but how does David, the psalm writer, respond (v 5-6)?

Having a newborn baby brings change and exhaustion. Emotions and hormones are running high (and low). You may feel you barely know yourself. Be encouraged: God knows you perfectly and his care for you is tailor-made. The writer does not find God's knowledge oppressive, but wonderful. Don't be afraid! Take refuge and shelter in God and his perfect, awe-inspiring knowledge.

• •

All-knowing Lord, I praise your wonderful, unsearchable knowledge. Thank you that you know everything about my character and my life. You know me better than I know myself, and therefore you are the One who can provide perfect care for me and my family. Help me to trust you, my Refuge and Shelter. Amen

10.
OUR EVER-PRESENT GOD

PSALM 139 v 7-12

⁵ You hem me in behind and before,
    and you lay your hand upon me.
⁶ Such knowledge is too wonderful for me,
    too lofty for me to attain.

⁷ Where can I go from your Spirit?
    Where can I flee from your presence?
⁸ If I go up to the heavens, you are there;
    if I make my bed in the depths, you
      are there.
⁹ If I rise on the wings of the dawn,
    if I settle on the far side of the sea,
¹⁰ even there your hand will guide me,
    your right hand will hold me fast.
¹¹ If I say, "Surely the darkness will hide me
    and the light become night around me,"
¹² even the darkness will not be dark to you;
    the night will shine like the day,
    for darkness is as light to you.

- Where is God (v 7-10)?
- Is darkness a barrier for God (v 11-12)?
- *Wherever* we are, what can we rely on (v 10)?

If we settle on the far side of the sea of nappies or (don't!) make our bed in the depths of exhaustion—God is there! Neither tiredness, nor mundanity, nor emotional or literal darkness can separate us from him. What deep joy and comfort this gives us!

....

Praise you, Father, that no circumstance or situation can separate me from you. Thank you that you are always there, whether I'm standing in front of the washing machine or feeding my baby in the night.

I pray for _____ , who is going through a dark time at the moment. Please help them to know that even darkness is light to you and you are the One who never leaves us, but holds us fast and guides us through. Amen

11.
OUR PERSONAL CREATOR GOD

PSALM 139 v 13-16

¹³ For you created my inmost being;
   you knit me together in my mother's
      womb.
¹⁴ I praise you because I am fearfully and
      wonderfully made;
   your works are wonderful,
   I know that full well.
¹⁵ My frame was not hidden from you
      when I was made in the secret place,
      when I was woven together in the
         depths of the earth.
¹⁶ Your eyes saw my unformed body;
   all the days ordained for me were
      written in your book
   before one of them came to be.

¹⁷ How precious to me are your thoughts,
      God!
   How vast is the sum of them!
¹⁸ Were I to count them,
   they would outnumber the grains of sand—
      when I awake, I am still with you.

o Why is the creation of a baby so significant (v 13-16)?

o Which parts of your baby has God created?

o What security does this give (v 16)?

These profound verses draw our gaze from the wonder of a baby to the glory of the God who knitted its body and wove its soul together. We don't know what our baby's life will hold, but we see here the loving power of the One who holds them.

....

Creator God, praise you for your intricate knowledge of my baby. Thank you that every day of their life is ordained by you. I pray for those whose babies have congenital disorders. May they know they are still created by you and have inmost beings that can respond to you. Amen

12.
OUR THOUGHT-FILLED GOD

PSALM 139 v 17-18

¹³ For you created my inmost being;
    you knit me together in my mother's
        womb.
¹⁴ I praise you because I am fearfully and
        wonderfully made;
    your works are wonderful,
    I know that full well.
¹⁵ My frame was not hidden from you
    when I was made in the secret place,
    when I was woven together in the
        depths of the earth.
¹⁶ Your eyes saw my unformed body;
    all the days ordained for me were
        written in your book
    before one of them came to be.

¹⁷ How precious to me are your thoughts,
        God!
    How vast is the sum of them!
¹⁸ Were I to count them,
    they would outnumber the grains of sand—
    when I awake, I am still with you.

The deeply personal context implies that these verses are, breathtakingly, referring to God's thoughts about us. As the English preacher CH Spurgeon said:

"That God should think upon us who are so poor and needy is the believer's treasure and pleasure … It is a joy worth worlds."

O How does David treat God's thoughts about him (v 17)?

O Can David measure God's thoughts (v 18)?

David cherishes God's intricately loving thoughts towards him so deeply that he falls asleep meditating on them, and wakes up with God's presence as his first comfort. He could also be talking about the ultimate awakening, from death. Even death cannot separate us from God.

• •

Father, give me great faith in your fathomless love for me. Although I'm a sinner who has done nothing to deserve your love, may I find great security in your thoughts about me being even more loving and abundant than mine for my baby. Amen

13.
THE SHOCK
OF SIN

PSALM 139 v 19-22

¹⁷ How precious to me are your thoughts,
     God!
   How vast is the sum of them!
¹⁸ Were I to count them,
     they would outnumber the grains of sand—
     when I awake, I am still with you.

¹⁹ If only you, God, would slay the wicked!
     Away from me, you who are bloodthirsty!
²⁰ They speak of you with evil intent;
     your adversaries misuse your name.
²¹ Do I not hate those who hate you, Lord,
     and abhor those who are in rebellion
         against you?
²² I have nothing but hatred for them;
     I count them my enemies.

²³ Search me, God, and know my heart;
     test me and know my anxious thoughts.
²⁴ See if there is any offensive way in me,
     and lead me in the way everlasting.

o How does David describe those who are not following God (v 19-22)?

o How do we know David loves God (v 21)?

These feelings and descriptions may sound extreme, even un-Christian, but we need to consider:

1. In his role as God's anointed king, David was a judge.

2. David is not writing out of superiority to sinners, but precisely because he knows he **is** a sinner. He is concerned to distance himself from the wicked so he will not get dragged away into rebellion with them.

3. We are shocked because we do not hold God's name and honour as highly as we should, and we do not see sin as dangerous.

....

Lord, please may my primary concern in life be your glory. Please give my child(ren) a passion for your name. Help my family to be wise in the friendships we make and to be set apart for you. Amen

14.
THE
WEIGHT-LIFTER

PSALM 139 v 23-24

[17] How precious to me are your thoughts,
    God!
  How vast is the sum of them!
[18] Were I to count them,
    they would outnumber the grains of sand—
    when I awake, I am still with you.
[19] If only you, God, would slay the wicked!
    Away from me, you who are bloodthirsty!
[20] They speak of you with evil intent;
    your adversaries misuse your name.
[21] Do I not hate those who hate you, LORD,
    and abhor those who are in rebellion
        against you?
[22] I have nothing but hatred for them;
    I count them my enemies.

[23] Search me, God, and know my heart;
    test me and know my anxious thoughts.
[24] See if there is any offensive way in me,
    and lead me in the way everlasting.

o Having explained God knows everything, how does this psalm finish (v 23)? Why?

You may be filled with anxious thoughts. As sleep deprivation bites, you're probably acutely aware of how offensive your ways can be to God (and others). But these final verses are a wonderful prayer of invitation to your all-loving Father:

to know you
to reassure you
to forgive and restore you
to lead you.

o What are you anxious about (v 23)?
o Where have you really mucked up recently (v 24)?

God wants us to open ourselves up to him. Of course, he knows everything already, but we need the joy and reassurance of unburdening ourselves to him and walking in his way.

••

Search me, God, and know my heart; test me and know my anxious thoughts. See if there is any offensive way in me, and lead me and my child in the way everlasting. Amen

15.
KID'S
PRAISE!

PSALM 8 v 1-2
**FOR THE DIRECTOR OF MUSIC.
ACCORDING TO GITTITH.
A PSALM OF DAVID.**

¹ LORD, our Lord,
   how majestic is your name in all the
      earth!
 You have set your glory
   in the heavens.
² Through the praise of children and infants
   you have established a stronghold against
      your enemies,
   to silence the foe and the avenger.

³ When I consider your heavens,
   the work of your fingers,
 the moon and the stars,
   which you have set in place,
⁴ what is mankind that you are mindful of
      them,
   human beings that you care for them?

In this psalm, David draws our eyes up to the sky, then back to the creation of the universe, and finally down to look beneath the heavens to the earth.

- **o** What does David call the Lord (v 1)?
- **o** Where can we see God's splendour (v 1-2)?

This psalm teaches that a child stuttering out a worship song is as eloquent for God as the wonder of the night sky! As parents, we pray we will nurture children who worship God. Verse 2 tells us this praise, inspiringly, is a powerful weapon against evil. Think how God could use something as seemingly insignificant as your child's praise to affect a non-Christian family member or friend for his glory.

••

LORD, our Lord, your name is majestic in all the earth.
I pray for _____ , who doesn't yet
know you, that through the praise of my child they
might be challenged to see your glory. Amen

16.
STARGAZING

PSALM 8 v 3-5
FOR THE DIRECTOR OF MUSIC.
ACCORDING TO GITTITH.
A PSALM OF DAVID.

³ When I consider your heavens,
    the work of your fingers,
  the moon and the stars,
    which you have set in place,
⁴ what is mankind that you are mindful of
      them,
    human beings that you care for them?
⁵ You have made them a little lower than
      the angels
    and crowned them with glory and
      honour.

⁶ You made them rulers over the works
    of your hands;
  you put everything under their feet:
⁷ all flocks and herds,
    and the animals of the wild,
⁸ the birds in the sky,
    and the fish in the sea,
    all that swim the paths of the seas.

Today, we see David, the writer, considering the heavens.

o What do we learn about God in verse 3?

o In light of God creating the universe, what is David amazed about (v 4)? Why?

o Where do we get our glory and honour from (v 5)?

The heavens were made by and belong to God, and so do we. In the grand scheme of all the galaxies and planets in the universe, we are miniscule—and yet God is mindful of us, giving us worth and dignity. We need to understand our significance in God's eyes, and yet be humbled in the knowledge that all we have comes from him and is for his glory.

••

Lord God, Maker of the heavens, thank you for your care for me and my family. Help me to raise my child to know how precious they are in your sight, but also to model humility before you. Amen

17.
FINDING
YOUR PLACE

PSALM 8 v 6-8
FOR THE DIRECTOR OF MUSIC.
ACCORDING TO GITTITH.
A PSALM OF DAVID.

³ When I consider your heavens,
   the work of your fingers,
 the moon and the stars,
   which you have set in place,
⁴ what is mankind that you are mindful of
      them,
   human beings that you care for them?
⁵ You have made them a little lower than
      the angels
   and crowned them with glory and
      honour.

⁶ You made them rulers over the works
      of your hands;
   you put everything under their feet:
⁷ all flocks and herds,
   and the animals of the wild,
⁸ the birds in the sky,
   and the fish in the sea,
   all that swim the paths of the seas.

God's world has a created order. We explore some of that order today.

- What position has God given us within his creation (v 6)?
- What can we learn about God from what he has given us (v 7-8)?
- Verse 9 repeats that God's name (not ours!) is majestic in all the earth. As rulers under God, how should we steward—manage as his appointed overseers—his creation?

As part of his creation, God gives children for us to enjoy, cherish and nurture. We are entrusted with their stewardship and care. We are to exercise loving and selfless authority over them, to ensure that they are like a well-tended garden: nourished, protected from invasive influences that would seek to destroy, and bringing glory to their Creator.

∙∙∙

Lord, thank you for your abundant generosity in giving us your whole creation to care for, under you. Help me be a godly steward of the world and my children. Amen

18.

LET US EXALT
HIS NAME TOGETHER

PSALM 34 v 1-7
OF DAVID. WHEN HE PRETENDED
TO BE INSANE BEFORE ABIMELEK,
WHO DROVE HIM AWAY, AND HE LEFT.

1 I will extol the LORD at all times;
  his praise will always be on my lips.
2 I will glory in the LORD;
  let the afflicted hear and rejoice.
3 Glorify the LORD with me:
  let us exalt his name together.
4 I sought the LORD, and he answered me;
  he delivered me from all my fears.
5 Those who look to him are radiant;
  their faces are never covered with shame.
6 This poor man called, and the LORD
    heard him;
  he saved him out of all his troubles.
7 The angel of the LORD encamps around
    those who fear him,
  and he delivers them.

This is one of the psalms written by David when he was running away from King Saul, who wanted him dead. David ended up behind enemy lines and his quick-witted self-defence strategy was to pretend to be insane.

- o What is David doing in v 1-3?
- o What has God done (v 4, 6-7)?
- o What is the wonderful truth in v 5?

Notice how David gives God all the credit for rescuing him. He doesn't boast about his clever plans or lightning-fast reflexes but glorifies the Lord for hearing him and saving him.

•••

Thank you so much, Father, that you are a glorious, powerful, loving and rescuing God. Deliver me from all my fears and help me to praise you. Thank you that although I'm ashamed of my sin, I can look to Christ for the joy of forgiveness. Hear this poor woman's prayers because of your precious Son. Amen

19.
LACKING NO GOOD THING

PSALM 34 V 8-14

⁸ Taste and see that the LORD is good;
blessed is the one who takes refuge
in him.

⁹ Fear the LORD, you his holy people,
for those who fear him lack nothing.

¹⁰ The lions may grow weak and hungry,
but those who seek the LORD lack no
good thing.

¹¹ Come, my children, listen to me;
I will teach you the fear of the LORD.

¹² Whoever of you loves life
and desires to see many good days,

¹³ keep your tongue from evil
and your lips from telling lies.

¹⁴ Turn from evil and do good;
seek peace and pursue it.

What do you really need at the moment? Sleep?! Help? Food? It may be hard to believe but there is something even better!

- o What does David advise us to do (v 8a, 9a, 10b)?
- o Why (v 8b, 9b, 10b)?
- o To "fear the Lord" (v 9, 11) means to remember that God is in charge and his opinion matters most. Why is this so hard?
- o What will it involve (v 13-14)?

Verses 13-14 sound fairly obvious, but isn't it so easy to fall into these kinds of sins when we are sleep deprived and grumpy? Especially with our nearest and dearest!

· ·

Please help me to take refuge in you daily, Lord. Teach me to be truthful and peace-seeking. Keep me from exaggerating or being argumentative especially when I am tired. Above all, help me to teach my children the fear of the LORD. Amen

20.
CLOSE TO US

PSALM 34 V 15-22

15 The eyes of the LORD are on the
    righteous,
        and his ears are attentive to their cry;
16 but the face of the LORD is against those
        who do evil,
        to blot out their name from the earth.
17 The righteous cry out, and the LORD
        hears them;
        he delivers them from all their troubles.
18 The LORD is close to the broken-hearted
        and saves those who are crushed in
        spirit.
19 The righteous person may have many
        troubles,
        but the LORD delivers him from them all;
20 he protects all his bones,
        not one of them will be broken.
21 Evil will slay the wicked;
        the foes of the righteous will be
        condemned.
22 The LORD will rescue his servants;
        no one who takes refuge in him will
        be condemned.

You will already have discovered that any little sound your baby makes has you awake and by their side in seconds. Isn't it amazing to think that is how God responds to our weakest cry?

- o What verbs describe God's actions in these verses? Underline them if you have a free hand!
- o How are the righteous described (v 18)?
- o Why might we be like that?

Wonderfully, all the blessings David lists are ours. And why? Verse 20 reminds us. It is quoted again in John 19 v 36 as Jesus died, so that we could be God's forgiven, righteous, cherished children.

....

Father, thank you that your eyes are upon me and your ears are attentive to my cries. Thank you that you are close to me, protecting and rescuing me. Most of all, thank you that, as Romans 8 v 1 puts it: "There is now no condemnation for those who are in Christ Jesus". Wow. Amen

21.
LISTEN TO ME

PSALM 78 V 1-4
A MASKIL OF ASAPH.

[1] My people, hear my teaching;
    listen to the words of my mouth.
[2] I will open my mouth with a parable;
    I will utter hidden things, things from
        of old—
[3] things we have heard and known,
    things our ancestors have told us.
[4] We will not hide them from their
        descendants;
    we will tell the next generation
  the praiseworthy deeds of the LORD,
    his power, and the wonders he has done.

It's one thing to hear and another to listen. Likewise it's easy to know something but not really let it sink in. Take some time to listen to this psalm for a few minutes now.

- What is Asaph, the psalm writer, wanting us to hear (v 1)?
- How has this message come to him and us (v 3)?
- What is the content of this teaching (v 4)?

Jesus' sacrificial death and awesome resurrection are the most praiseworthy and powerful deeds of the Lord.

....

Heavenly Father, thank you for your love, mercy and power in sending Jesus to suffer and die for my sins. Thank you for raising him to life and making me your child. Thank you so much for the people who faithfully passed on the good news of Jesus to me. Please help me to speak about your praiseworthy deeds, and your power and the wonders you have done, to someone today. Amen

22.
PASS IT ON

PSALM 78 v 4-6
A MASKIL OF ASAPH.

¹ My people, hear my teaching;
　　listen to the words of my mouth.
² I will open my mouth with a parable;
　　I will utter hidden things, things from
　　　of old—
³ things we have heard and known,
　　things our ancestors have told us.

⁴ We will not hide them from their
　　　descendants;
　　we will tell the next generation
　the praiseworthy deeds of the LORD,
　　his power, and the wonders he has done.
⁵ He decreed statutes for Jacob
　　and established the law in Israel,
　which he commanded our ancestors
　　to teach their children,
⁶ so that the next generation would
　　　know them,
　　even the children yet to be born,
　　and they in turn would tell
　　　their children.

God wants his people to know him. We have an amazing privilege and responsibility as parents to pass on the good news about Jesus.

- **o** Can/should we keep quiet about God's deeds (v 4)?
- **o** What did God want the Israelites to do (v 5)?
- **o** Why (v 6)?

Make talking about Jesus part of your daily life:

> *"Impress them* (God's commandments) *on your children. Talk about them when you sit at home and when you walk along the road, when you lie down and when you get up"* (Deuteronomy 6 v 7).

. . . .

Lord God, I ask that you would enable me to teach my children about you. Please equip me by your Holy Spirit and guard me against hypocrisy in my life. I also pray for children's and youth leaders at my church. Please help them to teach the children in our church family faithfully so that they would put their trust in you. Amen

23.
CHANGE
OF HEART

PSALM 78 V 5-8
A MASKIL OF ASAPH.

⁴ We will not hide them from their
   descendants;
   we will tell the next generation
the praiseworthy deeds of the Lord,
   his power, and the wonders he has done.

⁵ He decreed statutes for Jacob
   and established the law in Israel,
which he commanded our ancestors
   to teach their children,
⁶ so that the next generation would
   know them,
   even the children yet to be born,
   and they in turn would tell
   their children.
⁷ Then they would put their trust in God
   and would not forget his deeds
   but would keep his commands.
⁸ They would not be like their ancestors—
   a stubborn and rebellious generation,
whose hearts were not loyal to God,
   whose spirits were not faithful to him.

What is the goal of teaching our children about Jesus? Take a look.

o What did God command and why (v 5-6)?
o What three outcomes does God want in verse 7?
o What doesn't he want (v 8)?

Trust, recollection and obedience; or stubbornness, rebellion and disloyalty? By nature our hearts are full of the second list—even that angelic-looking baby of yours! Only by believing the good news that Jesus died to change our hearts can we live the life of verse 7. That's why it's such an important message to pass on.

....

Father, thank you that although my heart is naturally rebellious, stubborn and disloyal, Jesus dealt with all of that on the cross. Thank you that you give us a new heart and a new Spirit when we believe and trust in your Son. I pray you would perform that miracle in the life of my baby too. Amen

24.

A CRY
OF ANGUISH

PSALM 22 v 1-5
FOR THE DIRECTOR OF MUSIC.
TO THE TUNE OF "THE DOE OF THE
MORNING". A PSALM OF DAVID.

¹ My God, my God, why have you
forsaken me?

Why are you so far from saving me,
so far from my cries of anguish?

² My God, I cry out by day, but you do
not answer,

by night, but I find no rest.

³ Yet you are enthroned as the Holy One;
you are the one Israel praises.

⁴ In you our ancestors put their trust;
they trusted and you delivered them.

⁵ To you they cried out and were saved;
in you they trusted and were not put
to shame.

You may recognise the first line of this psalm. Jesus quotes it when he is dying on the cross.

- What is David doing in verses 1-2?
- Why is he so distressed (v 1-2)?
- What does he know about God (v 3-5)?
- Does what he knows match his circumstances?

It's one thing to know that God is there and that he is able and willing to help us, but sometimes it doesn't feel like that. David may have felt forsaken, but Jesus really was forsaken—so that we need never be, no matter how we feel!

....

Thank you so much, Father God, that Jesus went through the anguish of being separated from you on the cross so that I need never be. Thank you that nothing at all in all creation can separate me from the love of God in Christ Jesus. Amen

25.
TRUST IN
THE LORD

PSALM 22 v 6-11

⁶ But I am a worm and not a man,
     scorned by everyone, despised by
        the people.
⁷ All who see me mock me;
     they hurl insults, shaking their heads.
⁸ "He trusts in the LORD," they say,
     "let the LORD rescue him.
  Let him deliver him,
     since he delights in him."
⁹ Yet you brought me out of the womb;
     you made me trust in you, even at my
        mother's breast.
¹⁰ From birth I was cast on you;
     from my mother's womb you have
        been my God.
¹¹ Do not be far from me,
     for trouble is near
        and there is no one to help.

It can be hard to trust the Lord. In the uncertainty and hope of pregnancy or when your child is seriously ill. It's even harder when you are mocked by the world around you for doing so.

- o What is David going through (v 6-8)?
- o What does David recognise about God (v 9-10?)
- o So what does he pray (v 11)?

Even if you came to know Jesus later in life, you have been chosen by God since before the foundation of the world, so pray with David:

....

Lord, you brought me out of the womb; you made me trust in you, even at my mother's breast. From birth I was cast on you; from my mother's womb you have been my God. Do not be far from me, for trouble is near and there is no one to help. Amen

26.
SURROUNDED
BY ENEMIES

PSALM 22 v 12-18

¹² Many bulls surround me;
    strong bulls of Bashan encircle me.
¹³ Roaring lions that tear their prey
    open their mouths wide against me.
¹⁴ I am poured out like water,
    and all my bones are out of joint.
  My heart has turned to wax;
    it has melted within me.
¹⁵ My mouth is dried up like a potsherd,
    and my tongue sticks to the roof of
      my mouth;
    you lay me in the dust of death.
¹⁶ Dogs surround me,
    a pack of villains encircles me;
    they pierce my hands and my feet.
¹⁷ All my bones are on display;
    people stare and gloat over me.
¹⁸ They divide my clothes among them
    and cast lots for my garment.

David's words here point forward unmistakably to that first Good Friday. Take a look and wonder at what God went through for you.

- O What animal images does David use to describe these enemies (v 12, 13, 16)?
- O What effect does that have on the reader?
- O What similarities to the crucifixion can you spot? Underline them if you've got a free hand!

Handed over to his enemies—the physically violent, the mockers and gloaters, the indifferent. You may know these hymn words: "Ashamed, I hear my mocking voice call out among the scoffers". Jesus didn't just suffer instead of us; he suffered because of us.

••

Father, forgive me for my sins. I am sorry for the times I have been selfish, grumpy, unkind and ungodly today. Thank you that forgiveness is freely offered because of Jesus' willing self-sacrifice. Amen

27.
YOU ARE
MY STRENGTH

PSALM 22 v 19-21

¹⁹ But you, Lord, do not be far from me.
  You are my strength; come quickly to
  help me.
²⁰ Deliver me from the sword,
  my precious life from the power of
  the dogs.
²¹ Rescue me from the mouth of the lions;
  save me from the horns of the
  wild oxen.

²² I will declare your name to my people;
  in the assembly I will praise you.
²³ You who fear the Lord, praise him!
  All you descendants of Jacob, honour
  him!
  Revere him, all you descendants of
  Israel!
²⁴ For he has not despised or scorned
  the suffering of the afflicted one;
  he has not hidden his face from him
  but has listened to his cry for help.

When your baby cries they might mean "Help! Mum! I'm hungry" or "Help! Mum! I'm wet!" or "Help! Mum! I'm lonely". When we're in trouble, we cry out to the one who can help us.

- What does David ask for repeatedly in verses 19-21?
- What truth about God does he base his request on (v 19)?
- Do you think God answers him (see v 24)?

We don't know which deadly situation inspired this psalm, but God delivered David from it. Equally we know that Jesus' cries to his Father on the cross were unanswered (look back to verse 1). The people watching Jesus die said: "He saved others but he can't save himself!" But in reality, Jesus chose not to save himself so that he could save us.

....

Heavenly Father, thank you that you are my strength and you are never far from me because Jesus brought us together. Thank you that he was not rescued from death but rescued me by his death. Amen

28.
I WILL
PRAISE YOU

PSALM 22 v 22-24

¹⁹ But you, LORD, do not be far from me.
> You are my strength; come quickly to
> help me.

²⁰ Deliver me from the sword,
> my precious life from the power of
> the dogs.

²¹ Rescue me from the mouth of the lions;
> save me from the horns of the
> wild oxen.

²² I will declare your name to my people;
> in the assembly I will praise you.

²³ You who fear the LORD, praise him!
> All you descendants of Jacob, honour
> him!
> Revere him, all you descendants of
> Israel!

²⁴ For he has not despised or scorned
> the suffering of the afflicted one;
> he has not hidden his face from him
> but has listened to his cry for help.

You can't keep good news to yourself! Just think about the phone calls, texts, Facebook and Twitter announcements that went out from you and others when your baby was born.

- **O** In front of whom is David praising God (v 22)?
- **O** What does he want everyone to do (v 23)?
- **O** Why (v 24)?

Praise is always the response to rescue. David doesn't just keep it to himself—he wants everyone to know how great and compassionate the Lord is. He also wants everyone to praise God!

....

Father God, I praise and thank you that you have not hidden your face from me but have heard my cries for help. Thank you for saving me. Help me to rejoice in you with other Christians and to share the good news about your rescue with those who don't know you. In Jesus' name. Amen

29.
HE RULES OVER THE NATIONS

PSALM 22 v 25-28

²⁵ From you comes the theme of my
  praise in the great assembly;
  before those who fear you I will fulfil
  my vows.
²⁶ The poor will eat and be satisfied;
  those who seek the LORD will praise
  him—may your hearts live for ever!
²⁷ All the ends of the earth
  will remember and turn to the LORD,
  and all the families of the nations
  will bow down before him,
²⁸ for dominion belongs to the LORD
  and he rules over the nations.

²⁹ All the rich of the earth will feast and
  worship;
  all who go down to the dust will kneel
  before him—
  those who cannot keep themselves alive.
³⁰ Posterity will serve him;
  future generations will be told
  about the Lord.

David's praise isn't just limited to a local level; he's got the whole world in view!

o Where does David's praise start (v 25)?
o What is true of those who seek the Lord (v 26)?
o What will happen one day in the future (v 27)?
o Why (v 28)?

Philippians 2 v 10 reminds us that one day every knee will bow to Jesus. It starts now with those who fear the Lord (v 25), ie: those who recognise his kingship. But one day everyone will submit to God's rule because he is the Lord of all creation.

• •

Thank you so much, Father God, for the joy of living under your perfect rule. Father, I pray for people I know who don't yet acknowledge your rule—friends, family, people I bump into at mum and baby groups. Please help me to share the good news of living for ever with Jesus as King. Amen

30.
HE HAS
DONE IT!

PSALM 22 V 29-31

²⁷ All the ends of the earth
　　will remember and turn to the LORD,
and all the families of the nations
　　will bow down before him,
²⁸ for dominion belongs to the LORD
　　and he rules over the nations.

²⁹ All the rich of the earth will feast and
　　worship;
　　all who go down to the dust will kneel
　　before him—
　　those who cannot keep themselves alive.
³⁰ Posterity will serve him;
　　future generations will be told
　　about the Lord.
³¹ They will proclaim his righteousness,
　　declaring to a people yet unborn:
　　He has done it!

Well done for getting to the end of a long-ish psalm! What a brilliant note to end on.

- o What is hinted at in verse 29?
- o How long will the praise of the Lord last (v 30-31)?
- o What has the Lord done (v 31)?

While the Old Testament is pretty hazy on the details, there are wonderful hints of the eternal life promised in the New Testament (see verses 26 and 29). The praise of the Lord will last for ever, not just because we recount his deeds to each generation but because his people will live with him for ever.

"It is finished," Jesus cried.
"He has done it!" we reply.

••

Father God, I thank you and praise you for your righteousness and mercy. Thank you that Jesus paid the penalty for my sin on the cross so I could be forgiven. Please help me to tell my children (and grandchildren) about you. Amen

CASSIE
Q&A

Hard or easy labour? No.1 hard—three days, epidural, hideous. No. 2—gas and air, water birth, OK. No. 3—wrong position, painful, failed epidural but quick.

Best thing about parenting: Snuggling up in bed with all three of my sons in the mornings.

Worst thing about parenting: Poo. During potty training, my eldest "had an accident" at the doctor's and started smearing it all over himself while I was dealing with his screaming baby brother.

The hardest thing: Attempting (!) to keep my temper when I'm tired and everyone is shouting (or crying!) for my attention at once.

Best piece of advice: "Watch your baby, not the clock" if you're breastfeeding. My first baby was a super-speedy feeder and I wasted lots of energy worrying he wasn't getting enough milk.

Advice for the early days? Enjoy lots of newborn cuddles and concentrate on getting feeding right. Sleep will follow!

SARAH
Q&A

Best "male comment" from husband following forceps delivery, stitching and blood transfusion: "I've got this really painful spot behind my ear."

Best phone moment with doctor: "Your swab results are back: you need intravenous antibiotics before delivery." "Right, and what if I tell you I'm holding the baby right now?"

Biggest new mum inferiority moment: Neighbour with baby, same age as mine: "I've just finished my book..." (She's had time to READ A BOOK?) "I just need to compile the bibliography."

Before children I thought: I'm patient, calm and kind.

The hardest thing about parenthood: Loss of independence.

The best thing about parenthood: Each stage is better than the one before.

"AS LONG AS IT'S HEALTHY"

This is probably the prayer most often said during pregnancy. But my baby wasn't healthy. He was very ill and now has cerebral palsy. At the time it felt as if our dreams and our future were shattered, leaving us wondering where God was in all of it. People said well-meaning but unhelpful things; doctors didn't give the answers we needed; and we scrambled around for hope and sense. Where do you go from there?

I learned that Nathan was still my baby, fearfully and wonderfully made (Psalm 139) and a perfect gift from God. I really encourage you to hold on to that. He is no less made in the image of God because of his disability, and is a total joy and delight—even if it didn't feel like that in the beginning.

"Why?" is a question I did ask, and one that you can freely bring before the Father. He may not answer directly, but he does understand the pain behind the question. He saw his own child suffer, so he is no stranger to your helplessness and anguish. God loves your child deeply and completely.

Life with a significantly disabled child is never totally straightforward, but God's grace will step in and give you the strength you need for each day. As time goes by you will fall in love with your child, and life together will find its own rhythm.

There will also be surprises. Children have a tendency to prove doctors wrong and find their own way in the world. Nathan was supposed to be blind, and has generally surprised his doctors.

These children are resilient and beautiful whatever life throws at them. And the prayers and love of parents and others around them will make a difference in their lives. God has "plans to prosper you and not to harm you, plans to give you hope and a future" (Jeremiah 29 v 11)—and that includes your special child.

INGER

GOING IT ALONE?

Satinder has four children. She was married to a Sikh husband who was abusive towards her and her Christian faith. While pregnant with her fourth child, Satinder was hospitalised and realised she needed to end the relationship to protect her children from violence. With her husband in prison, she faced the birth of her daughter as a single parent. Here are some of her thoughts.

How did you feel facing motherhood as a single parent?

I was really depressed and down, almost suicidal really, but I don't know what I would have done without my faith and without God's people. They helped me: giving me advice, helping me with parenting, taking my older children to kids' clubs at church, and praying with me.

Some wonderful older Christian ladies have given me clothes and gifts for the children, been to court with me and helped me write letters. I asked: "Why do people help me so much?" and they replied that it's the Spirit of the Lord Jesus inside them.

What would you say to someone facing motherhood alone for whatever reason?

Never think that you are on your own! God is always with you. Go to church—his people will help you—and talk to him in prayer. Prayer is so powerful: we are talking to God himself and he will help you. You are never on your own!

What is life like now?

I can't express how much the Lord Jesus has done for me. He has been there for me in difficult trials. I'm free now; I don't live in fear. I can sleep and go to church and see my family—things I couldn't do before. I have a wonderful baby girl as well as my other children, who I love, and I want to bring them all up to know Jesus personally.

SATINDER

"DID YOU SAY TWINS?!"

"You've got your hands full!" Sound familiar yet?! For a parent with multiples (twins, triplets, quads…) there will be, at times, different highs and lows to those with singletons.

After having multiples, I found I was increasingly comparing myself to others. People would treat me as though I were saintly for "coping", while I would be thinking how rubbish I was doing and couldn't fit all I needed to into the day. It's been great to remember that God is not asking me to do as good a job as someone else. He's asking me to follow him as Lord and Saviour in the situation he has given me.

We have potentially more need of support from our church family. This is a great time to be served, and to learn more about God's grace and goodness. (If your church doesn't know you'd like help, tell them!) This blesses others as well as you. When some friends from church came and did a night shift for us, I literally cried with gratitude!

As multiple mums, we are more likely to come into contact with a wider range of health professionals, which offers a great opportunity to witness. We also have more strangers come and talk to us, intrigued by buggies overflowing with children. God can use all our conversations and quick comments in the street for his glory.

As they get older, you will have the blessing of many special multiple moments—but in the early days you may feel isolated as getting out can be harder, or health problems may mean baby groups aren't an option. But it does get better! At times when we're tired, or lonely, we can be reminded of Isaiah 40 v 31:

"Those who hope in the Lord will renew their strength. They will soar on wings like eagles; they will run and not grow weary, they will walk and not be faint."

BETH

NEW MUMS'
A-Z

Accept offers of help: babysitting, home-cooked meals, washing the dishes. Whatever it is, accept it! Don't be proud; people will want to help.

Bis for blessing (baptism or dedication or thanksgiving service). Whatever you choose to do, make thanking God for your child and committing them to him the focus. It can be a wonderful opportunity to share your faith with others.

Cis for church. Sometimes you'll ask yourself what is the point of going? You may be stuck in the crèche or a corridor, feeding and changing your baby for the whole service. Why not just stay at home with a nice coffee and listen to an MP3? Because church is the people and, believe it or not, you being there is a huge encouragement to other people. This season will pass, but persevere with it; you are serving others!

D "The Days are long but the years are fast." Motherhood has many repetitive aspects and can feel like Groundhog Day. But once your little baby is at school (eek!), you'll realise how precious those early years of their constant companionship and total dependence were. Seize it and treasure it because the cliché is true: it goes quickly.

E is for exercise. Try and take a daily walk with your baby. They will probably fall asleep and you will get some fresh air and exercise, which will do you good.

F is for feeding. Don't feel judged about how you feed your baby. People can get very intense and judgmental about this. Remember that it's God's opinion that matters, and just do what is best for you and your baby.

G is for guilt. Sometimes you will feel as if you are doing everything wrong. But you are a forgiven sinner in Christ Jesus. Don't forget that!

H is for humility. There are far too many bodily fluids involved in parenting. Dealing with them is a great lesson in humility!

Include your husband. Don't allow your love for your baby to push him away or de-skill him by not letting him help with baby things. Daddies are so important for children. If you don't have him around, make sure you involve uncles, brothers and grandads!

Jealousy of your husband's comparative freedom and independence since baby arrived can kick in. Get rid of it in prayer.

Keeping your house tidy? Forget it! Get people to help or just leave it.

L is for limitations. Feeling inadequate? You will. It's a great place to be. The Lord says: "My power is made perfect in weakness" (2 Corinthians 12 v 9).

M is for marriage. The most important thing for your child's emotional wellbeing is to see that mum and dad love each other. Prioritise your marriage. Benjamin Salk (family psychologist) says: "The greatest thing parents can do for their children is to love one another".

Never forget God's grace. You will fail your children, and your children may well fail you, but God's grace never will.

Order your loves rightly. Have no idols before God; that includes your children.

Post-natal depression. It affects over 10% of new mothers and is nothing to be ashamed of. It does not mean you are a failure as a mother or a Christian. Know the signs and get professional help.

Q is for "Quiet Times", when you read the Bible and pray. The dreaded Q word! God will give you those five spare minutes each day. Take them to read the Bible, not do the laundry.

Ration the amount of time visitors stay; protect your family time, and yourself from over-exhaustion.

S *inners raising sinners* is a realistic definition of parenthood. Apologise to your children when you get it wrong.

T is for tired! Remember that tiredness affects godliness.

University is not the goal of parenting—loving Christ is. When a child is saved, there is a whole lifetime ahead that can be used for God's glory.

Value your own parents more.

Wis for women's Bible studies. Daytime women's groups were an absolute lifeline for us in the churches we attended when our kids were babies. Such a blessing to be with other mums who understood what you were going through, and also older ladies with years of godly wisdom to share.

XKeep coming back to the cross.

You need to pray all the time. Especially when you're about to shout at your children.

Zis for Zzzzzzzzzzzzzzzzzzzzzzzzzzzzzzz. Try to sleep when baby does.

BEGINNING
WITH GOD

The *Beginning with God* range helps parents with young children to open up the Bible with their child and start them in a regular habit of reading God's word that will stay with them for life.

Beginning with God provides a simple way to start a pre-schooler in a regular habit of reading the Bible and growing to know God, who loves them. Read today's true story from the Bible; answer some simple questions; pray together; then stick in today's colourful sticker of the story.

Bake through the Bible helps parents with young children to explore the Bible with their child while having lots of fun cooking together. It contains 20 Bible stories, told in a simple, engaging style, that take your child through the whole storyline of the Bible. Each story is supported by a cooking activity that reinforces the main teaching.

UK: www.thegoodbook.co.uk/beginning
North America: www.thegoodbook.com/beginning
Australia: www.thegoodbook.com.au/beginning
New Zealand: www.thegoodbook.co.nz/beginning

thegoodbook
COMPANY
Opening up the Bible

At The Good Book Company, we are dedicated to helping Christians and local churches grow. We believe that God's growth process always starts with hearing clearly what he has said to us through his timeless word—the Bible.

Ever since we opened our doors in 1991, we have been striving to produce resources that honour God in the way the Bible is used. We have grown to become an international provider of user-friendly resources to the Christian community, with believers of all backgrounds and denominations using our Bible studies, books, evangelistic resources, DVD-based courses and training events.

We want to equip ordinary Christians to live for Christ day by day, and churches to grow in their knowledge of God, their love for one another, and the effectiveness of their outreach.

Call us for a discussion of your needs or visit one of our local websites for more information on the resources and services we provide.

UK & Europe: www.thegoodbook.co.uk
North America: www.thegoodbook.com
Australia: www.thegoodbook.com.au
New Zealand: www.thegoodbook.co.nz

UK & Europe: 0333 123 0880
North America: 866 244 2165
Australia: (02) 6100 4211
New Zealand (+64) 3 343 1990

ISBN 978-1-90955-911-0

PINK

ISBN 978-1-90955-981-3

BLUE